The
ABC's
and
123's
of Child Safety

By Sharon Blacknall

Illustrated by Linda Ray

To Contact Us:
Child Safety Tips and Programs™
P.O. Box 760458
San Antonio, TX 78245

Facebook – http://www.facebook.com/childsafetytipsandprograms.com
Twitter – http://www.twitter.com/childsafetyprgm

Inspiring Voices books may be ordered through booksellers or by contacting:

Inspiring Voices
1663 Liberty Drive
Bloomington, IN 47403
www.inspiringvoices.com
1-(866) 697-5313

Because of the dynamic nature of the Internet, any web addresses or links contained in this book may have changed since publication and may no longer be valid. The views expressed in this work are solely those of the author and do not necessarily reflect the views of the publisher, and the publisher hereby disclaims any responsibility for them.

ISBN: 978-1-4624-0437-7 (sc)
ISBN: 978-1-4624-0438-4 (e)

Printed in the United States of America

Inspiring Voices rev. date: 12/04/2012

NOTE TO PARENTS

Child Safety Tips and Programs™ is pleased to present "The ABC's and 123's of Child Safety" and "The All-Star Safety Patrol Kids" to parents and educators as an innovative tool to introduce children to the basics of safety while teaching them to count to 10 and their ABC's. Child safety education does not have to be scary nor should it be boring!

The book is broken down into two sections. The 123's of safety covers the basics every child should know as soon as possible. Children as young as two years old can start to learn the basic safety information presented. The key is repetition. Some parents review the information over meals or before bed. Other parents find that by making it fun like a game or song, the kids are motivated by the idea of earning their first certificate for a reward of your choice. Every child is unique and learns differently. It is up to you, as the parent, to determine the best method of teaching these very important safety rules. By the age of four, your child should be able to not only count to 10, but answer the associated questions with confidence.

The ABC's of safety introduces additional critical safety rules to children. As your child is introduced to each letter of the alphabet, a safety word and rule are also presented for you to discuss with them. Eventually, practicing safety will become as easy as ABC for your child! After mastering their ABC's and the associated concepts, your child will earn their second "Star" reward and officially be designated – "An All-Star Safety Patrol Kid!"

We believe all children deserve to grow up safe and unafraid. It is this belief that drives us to provide safety education that can be used to better prepare young children to face the dangers of the society we live in. We also want to salute the millions of parents, educators, child care providers and law enforcement officials that work tirelessly to keep children safe. We are honored to be of service to you all.

For additional safety tips and to download a free Child and Adult Safety Kit, go to – http://www.childsafetytipsandprograms.com

Let's keep our children safe together!

Thanks!
Sharon

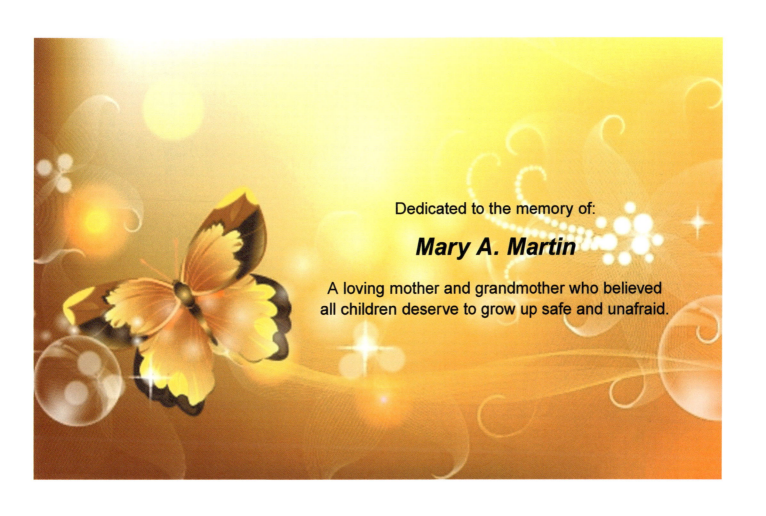

Dedicated to the memory of:

Mary A. Martin

A loving mother and grandmother who believed
all children deserve to grow up safe and unafraid.

Hi! We are the All-Star Safety Patrol Kids and we're here to teach you how to be safe. Are you ready? Let's get started!

Ryan

Samson

Faith

Anna

Matthew

Sophia

MY NAME IS

_____

I AM ____ YEARS OLD.

MY MOM'S NAME IS

_____

MY DAD'S NAME IS

_____

MY ADDRESS IS

_____

I LIVE IN

_____

(CITY, STATE)

MY PHONE NUMBER IS

_____

MY GRANDMA'S NAME IS

MY GRANDPA'S NAME IS

_____

MY BROTHER / SISTER'S NAME IS

_____

Certificate of Excellence

This certificate is awarded to

_____

for learning the 123's and Basic Rules of Safety!
You are now a Junior Safety Patrol Kid!

ANTS

Sophia says, "Do not touch **ANTS** or other bugs because they can bite or sting you!"

BULLY

Ryan says, "Anna! Don't be a **BULLY**! It's not nice to hit or be mean to others!
Be cool by being kind!" "I'm sorry, Ryan. I didn't mean to be a **BULLY**.
All-Star Safety Patrol Kids are ALWAYS kind and friendly to others."

CALL

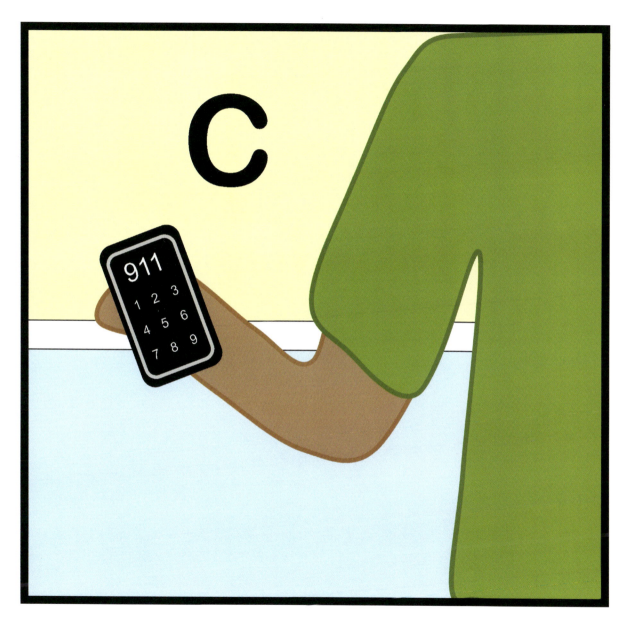

You should **CALL** 911 if there is a fire or emergency.

DOG

Samson says, "Do not pet a strange **DOG** without permission from Mom or Dad. All dogs are not friendly like me and they could bite you!"

ELECTRIC

If you stick your fingers or toys in **ELECTRIC** plugs, you will get zapped and it will hurt you!

FALL

Faith says, "Hold on to the rails when going up or down stairs so you don't **FALL** down!"

GIFTS

Matthew and Samson know that you should NEVER accept **GIFTS** or candy from people you don't know without permission from Mom or Dad!

HANDS

All-Star Safety Patrol Kids always remember to wash their **HANDS** before eating and after going to the bathroom.

IN

Just like Ryan and Sophia, you should always wear a seatbelt when riding **IN** a car.

JUMP

Faith got in trouble for not making good choices by jumping on the furniture. All-Star Safety Patrol Kids know that you don't **JUMP** on or off furniture, because you could fall and really hurt yourself!

KICK

If someone you don't know tries to grab you, you should fight back, **KICK**, scream loudly and try to run away!

LOOK

Matthew says, "If you are lost, **LOOK** for a Mom with
kids or a policeman and ask them for help."

MATCHES

All-Star Safety Patrol Kids do not play with **MATCHES** and neither should you! It is not safe! You could accidentally start a fire and someone could get hurt.

NO

"**NO** Sophia! I will not keep a secret from my Mom and Dad and neither should you!"
If anyone asks you to keep a secret from your Mom and Dad, just say <u>**NO**</u>!

OVEN

Anna says, "Do not play near or touch the **OVEN**. It is hot and can burn you!"

POOL

Samson says, "Always ask Mom or Dad for permission before getting into a **POOL**! Do not get in the water without an adult there to watch you."

QUIET

You should be **QUIET** like Matthew when your parents or teachers are talking to you.

RUN

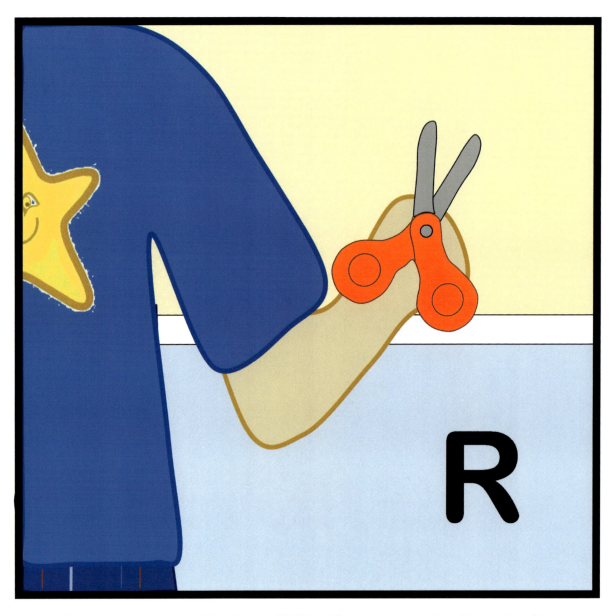

All-Star Safety Patrol Kids do not **RUN** with scissors and neither should you!
It is not safe because you could fall and cut yourself or someone else!

SICK

When you feel **SICK**, like Sophia does here, tell your Mom or Dad right away.

TEETH

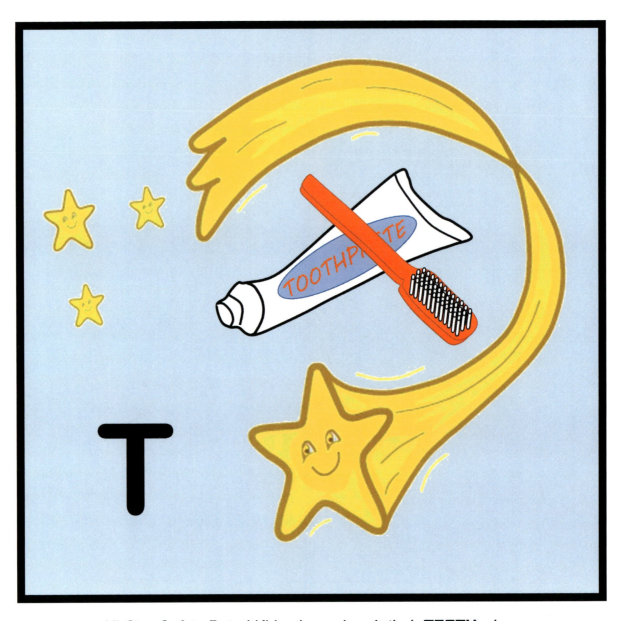

All-Star Safety Patrol Kids always brush their **<u>TEETH</u>** when they get up in the morning and before going to bed.

UNLOCK

You should never **UNLOCK** a door unless Mom or Dad says it's okay.

VAN

If someone driving a **VAN** or car pulls up beside you and tries to get you to get in, run away like Ryan and Samson are doing!

WAIT

All-Star Safety Patrol Kids never cross the street alone unless there is an adult present like a school crossing guard or policeman telling them when it is safe to cross. Always **WAIT** for an adult.

XYLOPHONE

Faith says, "Always pick up your **XYLOPHONE** and other toys so no one trips and falls."

YARD

When playing outside, All-Star Safety Patrol Kids do not leave the **YARD** without permission from their parents and neither should you! Stay together and stay close to the house.

ZOO

Anna says, "When visiting a **ZOO**, stay close to Mom and Dad. Do not wander off!"

Certificate of Excellence

This certificate is awarded to

_____

for learning the ABC's and 123's of Safety!
You are now an <u>All-Star Safety Patrol Kid</u> and can teach other kids about safety too!

CPSIA information can be obtained
at www.ICGtesting.com
Printed in the USA
LVIW02n1925050813
346415LV00001B